Christianity, Religion, Deception

THE PROCESS OF RECOGNIZING CHOOSING AND OBEYING

(Know My Voice VIII)

by

Rev. Dr. John Diomede

To order additional copies of this book, contact:

Proisle Publishing Services LLC
39-67 58th Street, 1st floor
Woodside, NY 11377, USA
Phone: (+1 646-480-0129)
info@proislepublishing.com

My Sheep Know My Voice

My sheep listen to my voice; I know them, and they follow me. I give them eternal life, and they shall never perish; no one will snatch them out of my hand.[1]

Jesus (Yeshua) of Nazareth

But as many as received Him, to them He gave the right to become children of God, *even* to those who believe in His name, [13] who were born not of blood, nor of the will of the flesh, nor of the will of man, but of God.[2]

The hour comes and now is that those truly submitted will worship the Father in spirit and in truth….The Father seeks such to worship Him. God is Spirit and those who worship Him must worship in spirit and in truth. [3]

Jesus (Yeshua) of Nazareth

"[10] "Even now the axe lies at the root of the trees. So that every tree that does not bring forth good fruit is cut down and cast into the fire.[4]

John (Yohanan) the Baptizer

---

[1] John 10:27-28 MW
[2] John 1:12-13
[3] John 4:23MW
[4] Mat 3:10MW

Table of Contents

Preface

All my writings use the terms *voices* and *hearing*. While there are records of God reaching into humanity's realm with an audible voice, it is rare. My employment of the terms *hearing*, and *voices* relates to the thought life of a person. We humans have thoughts, and those thoughts generally guide us in the decision-making journey of our lives. Those thoughts have a source. They are generated in our minds from four sources. I make no apologies for claiming the four sources of human thought because the knowledge of and the awareness of thought generation is vital to the life we experience in this realm. Let me say it another way. A thought is not nearly as important as its source. This truth can change your life. It is my sincere hope that you consider this subject matter seriously. It may bring you to a point of entry into a relationship that can help you discover the voice that you long to clearly hear. The voice that offers completeness. The voice that offers an existence born not of humanity but of God[5]. This is the voice of the Holy Spirit.

---

[5] But as many as received Him, to them He gave the right to become children of God, *even* to those who believe in His name, [13] who were born not of blood, nor of the will of the flesh, nor of the will of man, but of God. (Joh 1:12-13 NAS)

Introduction

Due to the proliferation of data, knowledge, and informational access, we live in a manipulative world. The ability to recognize accuracy or truth[6] is hindered due to mountains of contradictory data. And you can be sure that whatever information you are fed daily has been filtered according to the agenda of the one making it available. The concept that data arriving at one's doorstep has been filtered is not new. It has been going on since the beginning[7]. Is it possible to trust information when we are so familiar with contamination coming from an agenda-filled humanity? And the social media of today can be convincing. People not only say what they want, but often talk like experts on an array of topics, even when they themselves have not sufficiently researched the subject. Ideas, data, and so-called facts are restated without validation of accuracy. Because of the media platforms, talking heads say anything they choose, and it is taken in as fact by their

---

[6] 37 Pilate therefore said to Him, "So You are a king?" Jesus answered, "You say *correctly* that I am a king. For this I have been born, and for this I have come into the world, to bear witness to the truth. Everyone who is of the truth hears My voice." (Joh 18:37 NAS)

[7] Now the serpent was more crafty than any beast of the field which the LORD God had made. And he said to the woman, "Indeed, has God said, 'You shall not eat from any tree of the garden '?" (Gen 3:1 NAS)

supporters and the naive. So, we live in the world of opinion, and second-hand opinion at that. Opinion, not fact, drives our society. To the naïve human, this makes searching for and recognizing original sources boring, tedious, and inconsequential. All my books are about hearing directly from the Holy Spirit, The Source. God, if One exists, is The Source. The purpose behind this writing is to ask you to consider these questions. How can you follow God if you cannot hear God? How then can you recognize the voice of the Holy Spirit within your mind? And, if you cannot recognize that voice in your mind, how can you recognize it in another person? Lastly, if you cannot recognize God's voice, how can you adjudicate your actions? Let us take a stroll together down the road of relational experience above and beyond the limits of human opinion and conclusion as we examine the way to interact with the Holy Spirit and realize Truth directly from the source.

Cutting Through the Noise

Is it possible to hear God through the noise of the world and its opinions, especially through religion? The problem we are faced with is what a lawyer might call hearsay. In court, jurors must hear from the sources. In our world, one cannot properly accept or reject an ideology without receiving accurate information that they believe validates or repudiates the claim. This information must arrive in a raw state, unfiltered and from the source. And as in the case of a juror, personal ideology must not silence the voice of truth. But in real life, silencing the voice of the Holy Spirit often occurs. The opposing rationale first emanates from the deceptive voice of the demonic and is bolstered by the opinionated mob of the world. These opinions are what ultimately settles in the individual, primarily because they don't consider the source. One of the distractions is the noise of rationale. Humans have lost their ability to recognize truth because rationale redirects the path of truth. This occurs because recognition of truth can be uncomfortable. We can be challenged when we see how far off the path of sanity humanity has wandered, even recognizing it in ourselves. The rationalizing within politics, religion, healthcare, and finance heads up a host of contradictory, manipulative and distracting informational ideologies in our lives. My words may be hard to receive but the daily blatant demonstration of human hypocrisy should offer a reality check on the topic of our ability for recognizing, choosing, and obeying that which pulls us around by our nose ring every day, but it does not. Let me offer an example. The healthcare community has published contrary articles on so many related topics that I cannot begin to name them all. Coffee is a good example. No human can accurately conclude whether coffee is good or bad for us due to manipulated data that substantiates both sides of the argument. What is the truth? One side must be correct, but those who drink coffee don't care who is correct, they have become apathetic. The reason they don't care is because they just like their coffee, it satisfies a want. Such is the case with religion.

Most people accept what religion tells them about God without even a thought. Is it possible that people can know what God wants without religion? Is it possible that you can directly hear from and communicate with God without the help of religious leaders[8]? Is the Creator of the universe interested in you personally?

Communication from God happens all the time and humanity does not recognize it because humanity cannot cut through the noise of religion and the rationalization of human thought. Apathy has set into the process, even in what you might refer to as zealous religions because the only ones challenging religion are the atheists. Religion has made hearing directly from God just not that important. Why would one not need to hear from God directly? Because what we do know about God is usually enough. If God has something new to say, religion and religious leaders will hear and let people know. In the meantime, people go about living an illusion about God. They spend time complaining on their computers and cell phones about life and blaming God. They can also offer the occasional thank you to their deity when they are feeling magnanimous. Learning the voice of the Holy Spirit can cut through the noise of the world and disperse the fog of the demonic, but you must care enough to listen and be bold enough to change.

---

[8] 29 But Moses replied, "Are you jealous for my sake? I wish that all the LORD's people were prophets and that the LORD would put his Spirit on them!" (Num 11:29 NIV)

How Do You Like Your Coffee?

Years ago, if you entered a diner and ordered coffee you could be reasonably sure of what you would receive. Today, there is an infinite number of ways coffee can be served. When I enter a coffee chain and ask for a regular coffee, I get a dumbfounded look. They don't know what to do. As just mentioned, with all the focus on coffee, there has been a multitude of studies on the pros and cons of coffee's effect on the human body. Study after study contradicting each other. The researchers really don't mind contradicting data because it is their job. Additionally, contradiction has a usefulness in our world of opinion and marketing. Facts are manipulated, twisted, and turned to prove one conclusion or the other. Why? Because it offers a platform for gaining finances, name recognition and power. So how can one know what is true? Truth is no longer on the table; marketing is now the centerpiece, and the manipulators are expertly cagey. They know how to frame a topic, ask a question, or print an article title to keep their dynamic moving forward. I once read an article on the effects of a particular type of cardiovascular disease on people of color. The headline created fear and was inclusive of the entire referenced group. If you belonged to this group, the title instilled fear and gave you serious concerns about your health. After reading the article to the fourth page, they admitted that it affected less than ten percent of the group. But, if you did not read the article in full, you would spread opinion and fear, not fact.

You cannot know something unless you research that something. You must know the difference between fact and fiction. Only then can you draw a proper conclusion. And this is something you should want to do. I developed a taste for my coffee served a certain way and I developed a liking for my religion the way it was served to me. I did not ask the source because I did not know I would get a response. I am a medical professional. Yet, I wanted to know about God because the Holy Spirit was beckoning me. Thinking religion was the path, I studied for a long time, but recognition of God did not enter the picture until many years had passed, until I began to hear the Holy Spirit clearly. And until I began to believe direct hearing was possible. I had to empty my cup and fill it with the Holy Spirit.

Cognition

Cognition is defined using words such as the mental processes of knowing, of awareness, and of perception. How important is this to the course of our lives? This idea of cognition is foundational to both life and this writing. We live and learn daily. We fill our minds with the knowledge of that which interests us. We absorb information about politics, sports, religion, food, finance, science, art, and much more. When we find those topics that draw our attention, we compile data and regurgitate it regularly to relate to those around us who have similar interests or to inform those who do not. Humans have a desire to know, it makes us feel better and it also makes us appear more knowledgeable to ourselves and others. Cognition, combined with information, leads us down the road to recognition, learning and obedience. This process of cognition is interesting to me because as human beings grow, they collect data, perform rationalizations, draw conclusions, and develop obedience to those conclusions. Therefore, they become subordinate to or resistant to various ideologies. All this occurs due to cognition. This process, and our very existence, hinges on that which occurs in our mind. This process is thoughts, or voices, populating the unseen arena of the mind and doing battle with each other until a winner emerges in our life. That of which I speak are the four voices of our realm. The experience of our existence opens us up to hearing these four voices. Voices which bring us to the doorstep of recognizing, of choosing, of obeying. We witness every day individuals living out their existence in obedience to something. As we participate, let us seek to hear and obey the one voice that guides us to live our existence compassionately, mercifully and with forgiveness. This is the voice of the Holy Spirit.

Cognition Must Precede Obedience

Cognition is our ability to comprehend life. Humans are mostly successful in comprehending life, so why do we fail to comprehend communication from God? Human cognition demonstrates the broken conduit to the voice of God. Data both helps and hurts the process of human cognition as it relates to the process of hearing God. Humanity was able to figure out the idea of schooling, learning, and doing. Through the process of learning, we can better understand a topic. Performing virtually any job takes a process of learning and understanding. One of the most complex professions is that of a surgeon. The medical profession has determined that the process to attain full status of surgeon can go well into a person's thirties. The surgeon must understand the complexity of the human body. Their cognition offers the ability to recognize what is proper procedure or not, what is healthy and what is disease. Their wrong choices can kill another human being. Another two complex professions are psychiatry and psychology. These individuals must receive verbal data from the mind of another human who is in trouble, stressed, afraid, hurt, and broken. But this patient is seeking these professionals' help to solve a problem emanating from an unseen place, an unseen source. Recognizing disease is not so easy. Unlike the surgeon, the entire profession is built on data that comes from the mind. The surgeon can see a tumor, but the psychiatrist does not have the same luxury. Yes, we can see and understand the physical brain and its chemicals, but we cannot see how it thinks. We cannot see the root of an emotional tumor and cut it out. But together with the Holy Spirit, surgery can occur and we can cauterize the source of the spiritual, psychological, and emotional bleeding. This is the unseen process of hearing the voice of the Holy Spirit. Jesus said we could not see the Holy Spirit, but we would know the Presence[9]. Most lay people don't know that Jesus of Nazareth grew in awareness of who he was, his mission and purpose. He was not laying in the manger with full awareness of being the Messiah[10]. He experienced personal revelation from the Holy Spirit ultimately bringing him to the cross and our deliverance. His disciples recorded many of the events of his life. The

---

[9] the Spirit of truth. The world cannot accept him, because it neither sees him nor knows him. But you know him, for he lives with you and will be in you. (Joh 14:17 NIV)

[10] And Jesus grew in wisdom and stature, and in favor with God and man. (Luk 2:52 NIV)

bible says He learned obedience by being fully human[11].
As he recognized, he grew in awareness. Knowing preceded understanding and obedience.

Cognition is a part of the human learning process. One must receive the information before they can act. This process was true for Jesus, and it is true for all other humans. One cannot be obedient to the voice of God unless they hear the voice of God. Let me repeat. It is impossible to be obedient to God unless one hears from God! Not from an organization. Not from another human. These can offer direction, but they can never relay cognitive truth Spirit to spirit because "Truth" is an experiential interaction that can only occur with the Holy Spirit. I have a friend who asked me which one of my books could help her. As she began to read the book I selected, she experienced cognitional truth. Information that came from the voice of the Holy Spirit. How do I know this? After she began reading, she said, "What you're suggesting in your writing is really hard!" My writings simply suggest obedience to the voice of the Holy Spirit Who suggests simple principles such as

---

[11] [8] Although He was a Son, He learned obedience from the things which He suffered. [9] And having been made perfect, He became to all those who obey Him the source of eternal deliverance, (Heb 5:8-9 NAS)

patience. She is a good religious person. But all her experience and obedience are the result of the voice of an organization, the voice of the world. She can follow those rules, such as going to church, but they still leave her in a quandary because it does not fulfill relational truth of obedience to God, only obedience to an organization which can never fill relationship. It was the voice of the Holy Spirit that awoke her cognition of truth, and a sense of conviction, a sense of challenge, a sense of brokenness. It is that same voice that will orchestrate the victory of patience in her life. On her own she experienced Truth and on her own she will learn discipline as the Holy Spirit speaks with her. But she must not let the other voices distract her with rationale and data. The presence of the Holy Spirit[12] compassionately told her she was broken. When the voice of God breaks through, one is challenged in a way that this world cannot produce. The challenge is to change on the inside, which as she said is hard. Truth called out in her mind to "hear/listen". The Hebrew *Sh'ma* calls Israel, and all people, to hear or listen to God's voice. Once heard, unless callousness has set into

---

[12] "But when He, the Spirit of truth, comes, He will guide you into all the truth; (Joh 16:13 NAS)

the heart, that call of truth is more real than any sound, thought or event in life. It awakens one's spirit. Its robustness reveals the emptiness of religion. This awakening, or light, can bring a person along the path of obedience to God because the message from God is experienced and the sense of aloneness is interrupted. Depending on the amount of truth we accept will light and determine our path toward The King. And this is the only path that matters. Whatever gifts, knowledge, ability, or expertise you have been given; Whatever weakness, disability, challenge, or distraction you have in this life all are yours to navigate this road, the road to The King. It all starts with cognition and culminates in obedience to The King, not to some organization, person, vocation, or thought that emanates from a human source – and there are plenty, but from the Holy Spirit. Organizations and leaders can only tell you what they think about God, but God can speak to you directly about Himself.

The Point of Entry

Now you might say to me, "John, can every religion and religious denomination be wrong?" The purpose of my writings is not to direct you to or from earthly organizations, it is for you to become familiar with the guidance from the Holy Spirit as promised by the Messiah. I never encourage people to leave their current organization or change based on my words. That would simply create another false point of entry in their life. I will say it again, "stay where you are unless, or until, the voice of the Holy Spirit leads you to the next chapter of your life". When Abraham heard the voice of God[13], he began a new chapter, a new point of entry. Leaving his family must have been a challenge but I can assure you it was not as challenging as being contacted by The Creator.

Every phase of life has some point of entry. Humans are born and, depending on the place, culture, nationality, race, gender and more, they enter a process whereby they begin to experience this life, this reality, this realm. That entry takes us on some path, a path of

---

[13] Now the LORD said to Abram, "Go forth from your country, And from your relatives And from your father's house, To the land which I will show you; (Gen 12:1 NAS)

being Muslim, Christian, Jewish, Hindu, or other religion. It is a path of being Russian, British, Japanese, Korean, Asian, African, Australian, American, Latino and many others. In most cases, these are the building blocks of the entrance to the individual's life in this realm. Then they begin to accumulate data, relationships, and experience. They begin to contemplate matters pertaining to financial, political, sociological, medical, academic, religious, and spiritual understandings. Based on their conclusions, they form other entry points on their life's journey and embrace the complex reality in which they live.

One of those entry points takes us through the door of the idea, knowledge, and being of God. I am not referring to religion. Religion is not the entry point to contact with God. It has never been and cannot ever be. Why? Because religion is a man-made phenomenon of this realm. It is like politics and finance. It has no door, no entry point to the next realm. Religion can even be sourced from the demonic[14]. You may say to me, "Your foundational book is the Bible, so what of Moses and the

---

[14] 21 And Elijah came near to all the people and said, "How long *will* you hesitate between two opinions? If the LORD is God, follow Him; but if Baal, follow him." But the people did not answer him a word. (1Ki 18:21 NAS)

religion he started"? Moses did not start a religion. Had Moses remained in Egypt as a prince and political leader, he surely would have started a religion. In fact, politics and religion are very closely related. Moses was removed from the religio-political environment of Egypt and relocated to a place where he could be introduced to God. Prior to Moses fleeing to Midian, it was Moses' conscience that led him to defend the Israelite and kill the Egyptian. But conscience is different than the voice of the Holy Spirit. The conduit to the Holy Spirit that came from Jesus had not yet been established[15]. Currently, the only door to the next realm, except death, exists directly through the human being. So, for Moses, there was about to become a new point of entry into a new relationship. To quiet the voices of deception, God waited forty years to make that introduction. During those forty years, I believe Moses realized he was alone, and that is when the Voice of God broke through the silence and reached out to Moses from the burning bush. In those forty years through silence Moses became acquainted with his own brokenness[16]. That self-aware brokenness

---

[15] By this He (Jesus) spoke of the Spirit, whom those who believed in Him were to receive; for the Spirit was not yet *given*, because Jesus was not yet glorified. (Joh 7:39 NAS)

[16] (Now the man Moses was very humble, more than any man who was on the face of the earth.) (Num 12:3 NAS).

is revealed when Moses urges God to send someone else[17]. The remnants of being a prince in Egypt had no place in his mind. People think that seeing a burning bush would make them follow God. Moses told us differently[18]. He wanted all the people to hear God. When God broke into this realm and spoke to Moses, Moses began to realize he was not alone and deliverance of the Israelites, a family, his family, was also on God's mind. It took a little coaxing, but Moses went back for his people, his family and the relationship. God was the authority and power behind Moses[19], but the people did not understand that idea. God wanted the people to hear His Voice directly, yet they refused[20]. God wanted to be their King, but many in Israel never got the message. Moses knew this and foretold them that they would follow other gods and other religions, once settled in the Promised land[21]. God wants relationship and the Holy

---

[17] But Moses said, "Pardon your servant, Lord. Please send someone else." (Exo 4:13 NIV)

[18] 29 But Moses replied, "Are you jealous for my sake? I wish that all the LORD's people were prophets and that the LORD would put his Spirit on them!" (Num 11:29 NIV)

[19] 21 Then Moses stretched out his hand over the sea, and all that night the LORD drove the sea back with a strong east wind and turned it into dry land. The waters were divided, (Exo 14:21 NIV)

[20] They stayed at a distance 19 and said to Moses, "Speak to us yourself and we will listen. But do not have God speak to us or we will die." (Exo 20:18-19 NIV)

[21] For I know how rebellious and stiff-necked you are. If you have been rebellious against the LORD while I am still alive and with you, how much more will you rebel after I die! (Deu 31:27 NIV)

Spirit is that point of entry, that conduit, made possible by and promised by Jesus the Messiah for each of us to experience that relationship.

Religion today continues to be what it was since the beginning of time, an entry point to distraction for humanity and a way for broken humans to feel better about themselves, but it does not accomplish healing the human mind. But humanity does not see it that way because of apathy. They see following the tenets of religion as a way of getting God's approval. They see it as a way of checking off another one of the boxes of this life to appease their conscience, a conscience put there by God and dulled by rationale. Deception is the design of religion because it shrouds the connection to God in secrecy. The deception of religion is the promise that when this life is over the next awaits with no consequences to hate, anger, and a merciless human heart. Religion offers the promise of making it to the next realm without a life of compassion, mercy, and forgiveness. People accept their religion at face value, never asking any of the most relevant questions about their actions and thoughts. This is the point of entry into deception.

The life activities of a human are very related to their point of entry into their current thoughts, opinions, and interests. One must examine their life daily. One must understand how they made it to where they are and survey their choices, understand their navigation, and realize how they are living life. People I speak to have a huge spiritual and emotional void. They have many unanswered questions. And they have major concerns about where they will be headed when they depart this realm. These thoughts can only be addressed by the Holy Spirit. Seeking the voice of the Holy Spirit is the only point of entry to eternal security. God promises to reach out to anyone who seeks The Presence[22]. The Father sent Jesus to orchestrate this experience and manage the relationship[23]. Personal contact with Jesus through the Holy Spirit is the point[24] of entry, not religion.

---

[22] 'Call to me and I will answer you and tell you great and unsearchable things you do not know.' (Jer 33:3 NIV)

[23] "Do not let your heart's be troubled. You believe in God; believe also in me. 2 My Father's house has many rooms; if that were not so, would I have told you that. I am going there to prepare a place for you? (Joh 14:1-2 NIV)

[24] 7 Therefore Jesus said again, "Very truly I tell you, I am the gate for the sheep. (Joh 10:7 NIV)

Echad Relationship and Aloneness

In my previous books, I speak of *Echad*. Jesus spoke of it also. He said; he and the Father were One and we could be One with him also. Let me refresh your memory about the *Echad*. There is a Christian doctrine that denominates God's being as the "Holy Trinity". This doctrine originates from the biblical record where Jesus indicates that he, the Holy Spirit and The Father exist as One Unity, *Echad*. The Hebrew word *Echad* means Unity. This compound oneness can be compared to your body, your mind, and your emotions. They are distinct in action, for example hunger, cognition, and fear but all are contained in one unit and work as one. The idea of *Echad* originates in the Tanakh (Old Testament). In the Hebrew Sh'ma, God claims Being with the word Echad. "Hear O Israel, the Lord your God, the Lord is *Echad*, One, a Unity. Maimonides[25] refers to God's Unity in his tenets. Religion cannot accept the bible at face value so, it must attempt to explain everything. It creates doctrines such as the one on the trinity to explain this

---

[25] "I believe with perfect faith that G-d is One. There is no Unity that is in any way like His. He alone is our G-d. He was, He is, and He will be" Kaplan, Aryeh. The Fundamentals of Jewish Faith. New York: National Conference of Synagogue, 1975.

phenomenon. This makes the leadership appear more knowledgeable about God so the organization bolsters its spiritual prowess while gaining respect and adherents. Hence, there are many doctrines like the one on the trinity. Organizations such as the Jehovah's Witnesses' have their own dogma which rejects the trinity doctrine. Judaism also rejects this doctrine. I will not delve into the complexity of either theology. It suffices simply to state that God's Unity exists as a relationship and is defined by the Hebrew _Echad_.

So, doctrines aside, Jesus simply points out this Unity and claims it is the relationship of himself, the Holy Spirit, and The Father, he never offers a definition. While we cannot either define or understand the Being of God, the point of this chapter is not to make more doctrine, it is the idea of this connection, this Unity.

The most significant fact is the Unity of God offers a fix for broken humanity. In my other writings, I reference the inescapable fact that we are alone. When all the distractions and activities calm down, we can realize that there is no one else inside of our mind with us. This makes the mind a veritable playground for the exposure it experiences to the voice of the demonic. I say playground because most humans are not able to or do not care to assign designation to their thoughts, the voices, so like a carousel their thoughts go around and around. While we can experience all four voices, the voice of self, the voice of the world, the voice of the demonic and the voice of the Holy Spirit, fear is the primary weapon of this demonic voice, and it is proliferated by the voice of the world. But people have trouble understanding that the voice of self, guided by the voice of the Holy Spirit, can resist the urges of the other two voices. Freewill allows us to choose which thoughts to validate. While the input arises from the four sources, the choosing process is made in the solemnity self. We use our free will to choose. One of the greatest gifts we were given was freewill. None of the voices can choose for us, only the voice of self. Freewill allows us to choose the actions that stem from our mind. As we live our lives, the single most crucial factor in this process is to define the source of the voice, the source of the thought and not allow demonic or worldly voices to referee a game on our home field. The process of learning and data collection can offer guidance, but, again, the choice is made in our aloneness under the auspice of our being's freewill. God gave humanity a conscience to assist in this process. The bible records this in the story of Noah. The Voice of God reached out to Noah. Noah chose! Human survival came down to one man's conscience and ability to recognize and obey God. But conscience can become scarred, dull, and unresponsive[26].

God being faithful, continued to reach out to humanity throughout time and culminated that reach in Jesus of Nazareth, The Messiah. Jesus sends the Holy Spirit to help guide people, to assist our conscience. As recognition grows, so does the voice of the Holy Spirit. As the voice of the Holy Spirit grows, we have a better idea of what God wants us to do or not. This process is challenging and the routine shortcut, religion, must be avoided. If entered, this is the _Echad_ relationship of which Jesus spoke[27]. While conscience is us, the Holy Spirit is not us. The Holy Spirit becomes the company for our aloneness and the cheering section for conscience. Recognizing the Spirit's voice occurs in our aloneness and unity with the Holy Spirit can be realized. And so, we are no longer alone as the journey to our completeness moves further along.

---

[26] 2 Such teachings come through hypocritical liars, whose consciences have been seared as with a hot iron. (1Ti 4:2 NIV)

[27] that all of them may be one, Father, just as you are in me and I am in you. May they also be in us so that the world may believe that you have sent me. (Joh 17:21 NIV)

The Voice of God

Some might argue that they are good religious people following the mandates of their religion or religious organization. And so, it is with this claim that the "rubber meets the road". What do I mean by "rubber meets the road?" Traction or friction occurs when thoughts are converted into actions. When performing deeds of religion, the conscience of the individual allows them to feel justified or validated because of religious adherence. Religion and religious organizations are full of commandments, laws, and regulations. It is why we have feasts, holidays, and holy days. In addition to the bible, and its many translations, there exists mountains of extra-biblical material such as the Talmud, Mishnah, The Book of Mormon, and Christian bible commentaries. And there are the holy books of Islam, Buddhism, Hinduism, and more. All these writings provide the guard rails of security for humans to develop a sense of religious validation and, in some way, honor their respective deity. Additionally, the claim might be made that God chooses representatives to speak for Him, which is also valid but has little value when compared to the actual voice of the Holy Spirit.

On the other side, the communities of the irreligious, agnostics and atheists would ask, "since each of these writings were recorded by people, why waste your time assuming some unseen deity made these claims or requires these efforts?"

If a person cannot hear directly from the source, there exists a void or disconnect. The Bible makes us aware that God knows this fact[28]. There are various places in the bible that suggest a voice came directly out of the sky or heaven[29]. The Bible also tells us of the story of Moses and the burning bush from where God spoke. So, hearing directly from the source would put all religious arguments to rest. People would surely believe in, and follow God if they heard directly, or would they[30]?

Jesus said his followers would hear directly from God, the Holy Spirit. Furthermore, that communication

---

[28] "This is the covenant I will make with the people of Israel after that time," declares the LORD. "I will put my law in their minds and write it on their hearts. I will be their God, and they will be my people. (Jer 31:33 NIV)

[29] He fell to the ground and heard a voice say to him, "Saul, Saul, why do you persecute me?" 5 "Who are you, Lord?" Saul asked. "I am Jesus, (Act 9:4-5 NIV)

[30] For this is what you asked of the LORD your God at Horeb on the day of the assembly when you said, "Let us not hear the voice of the LORD our God nor see this great fire anymore, or we will die." (Deu 18:16 NIV)

would be a direct message from Jesus and The Father[31]. What do you think is the purpose of Jesus' words? It stands to reason that this communique from The Father and The Son would offer us help in our decision-making process. Is what Jesus said possible? How do we know we are not just fabricating thoughts? Why would we need some unseen, and possibly unverifiable, source reaching out to us when we have all the writings I mention above. Writings that many "holy" men and women validated. I don't know of one mainline religion that encourages hearing directly from the next realm without help. To complicate the matter, there are psychics and mediums who act as conduits to that realm. Who are they speaking with and is it real? Contact is not only possible, but it occurs because broken and alone humans long not to be alone. Jesus of Nazareth said that God will contact you and He would not use another person. He is saying you don't need to go through human conduits because God, the Holy Spirit, will help you directly. God will fill your aloneness

---

[31] "But when He, the Spirit of truth, comes, He will guide you into all the truth; for He will not speak on His own initiative, but whatever He hears, He will speak; and He will disclose to you what is to come. (Joh 16:13 NAS)

with the His presence. He, the Holy Spirit, will guide you![32]

This guidance is very different than the religious materials mentioned above and the advice of psychics. In some cases, it sounds very similar. And consider this thought; In all cases, communication from the Holy Spirit will be validated by biblical content, even if a person has had no contact with or knowledge that the bible even exists. I share a story on this exact situation at the end of the book. Hearing from God is very different than hearing from humanity. God's effect on every biblical personality altered their path, their life, and their existence. They experienced a profound humility. They sacrificed everything about themselves for this journey. Some, like John the Baptist, for certain periods of time, sacrificed the company of humanity for the companionship of the Holy Spirit. Sometimes we need to ditch the other three voices so we can focus on the Holy Spirit. I mentioned in another writing how I will turn on the television and mute the voice because I am in constant conversation with the Holy Spirit. The television is just noise from the world. Biblical

---

[32] But when he, the Spirit of truth, comes, he will guide you into all the truth. (Joh 16:13 NIV)

personalities displayed many varied examples of _Echad_ relationship. King David, in Psalm 51 states the sacrifice acceptable to God is a broken spirit and a contrite heart[33]. He heard this through relationship with the Holy Spirit. But religion has people too busy attempting to reproduce some other person's experiences instead of embracing and living out their own journey. The voice of humanity requires money and actions to promote the organization. The voice of the Holy Spirit satisfies the individual with the thought that God is more interested in what He can do for them that what they can do for Him. It is possible to hear this voice no matter what your condition, no matter what your religion, no matter what your past or present situation. You probably have heard the Holy Spirit and are not even aware of that moment. The Holy Spirit will guide you to a good place. It will not be a political place, it will not be a social justice place, it will not be a religious place. But it will take an effort on your part. The guidance of the Holy Spirit will displace your current journey or the lack of a journey. Your eyes will be opened to vast wasteland of aloneness that imprisons

---

[33] The sacrifices of God are a broken spirit; A broken and a contrite heart, O God, You will not despise. (Psa 51:17 NAS)

humanity when you hear the Voice of God, once you experience true companionship, *Echad* companionship. This is the voice of the Holy Spirit.

Organization vs Entity

Over the course of human history, there have been many houses of worship, religions, and gods. I know many people who are devoted, even nominally, to their organization, an organization which, in most cases, claims to represent God. These organizations have processes and procedures that they assert came from their god and are performed to honor that god. Religious practice is referred to and represented by liturgy, holy days, holidays, dogma, etc. Most religions existing today have existed for centuries. These organizations are led by men and women that seem to have a calling to help people who follow that god/organization. Religious organizations are comprised of people attempting to perform a process related to and required by their god. The leaders of these organizations not only represent the organizations' god but can also get direction from their god, which occurs mostly through interpreting historical data and documents. And in some cases, they do claim direct interaction. Humanity, at large, is ok with this process because they don't like an empty coffee cup, so they accept what is served to them.

Through historical documents, events, recordings and more, these leaders move the organization along.

These organizations can be large or small. They can have adherents numbering in the single digits to the tens of thousands and millions. Some collect and spend billions of dollars to potentiate the causes of their organization. Some causes support people in need but there is a plethora of other causes related to varied topics with which these organizations work. Lay adherents and leaders may speak out against competing organizations, but for the most part, they simply are concerned with their own group because it pays the bills. When people are approached by representatives from another group about beliefs or membership, many will say, "you believe what you believe, and I will believe what I believe". This position emanates from the demonic voice. This voice makes the claim that faith is a very personal subject. The source of this manipulation is fear, and the amusement park is the human mind. Jesus never entertained this thought. He made faith public. The manipulation that faith is personal shuts down all conversation on the topic. Additionally, people will rarely entertain the thought of visiting or moving to another organization for many reasons. I have enumerated them in my last book, The King, The Kingdom, The Citizens.

There is an old saying, you can't see the forest through the trees. It is the very existence of organization that blocks the view of God and replaces the voice of God. If God exists, then like us, He is alive. He is a being. The bible says God is Spirit[34]. To our mind, this makes a statement. It represents God's being. The bible says God created humankind in His image and likeness[35]. I don't think appearance is the issue. I believe the unseen is the issue, life is the issue, entity is the issue. An entity is something that exists apart from its physical properties. God is an alive[36] entity and therefore we are alive entities, the difference is we had a beginning. That said, we are more than our physical body. All the philosophers throughout history speak to the fact we humans exist and that we are alive! The bible claims we have life. Humanity, in various legal systems and

---

[34] God is spirit, and those who are submitted to Him must worship in spirit and truth." (Joh 4:24 NAS)

[35] Then God said, "Let Us make man in Our image, according to Our likeness; and let them rule over the fish of the sea and over the birds of the sky and over the cattle and over all the earth, (Gen 1:26 NAS)

[36] And God said to Moses, "I AM WHO I AM"; and He said, "Thus you shall say to the sons of Israel, 'I AM has sent me to you.'" (Exo 3:14 NAS)

documents, has defined that we have life. The bible further stipulates that our life is in The Life, Jesus[37].

Our life, our entity is unseen. This is where the Holy Spirit enters the conversation. Jesus said something that confounds the biblical community. I say confounds because it is a statement that cannot be proven existentially. He claimed that he and the Father are One and he further claimed that we could be One with Him. This, again, is the Hebrew word *Echad*. Once again, we encounter this Entity, this Unity that exists as God. The *Echad* permeates everything via the Holy Spirit. Since humanity exists in God, humanity has the opportunity to never be alone, unless one chooses being alone[38] by rejecting God. People have said to me they don't reject God. They want God. But they want the god they have made up. Religions' god is defined by humanity. God defines Himself during the personal relationship with the individual. God cannot be defined without relationship. We have examples of this throughout the

---

[37] That which was from the beginning, which we have heard, which we have seen with our eyes, which we have looked at and our hands have touched--this we proclaim concerning the Word of life. (1Jo 1:1 NIV)

[38] The Son of Man will send forth His angels, and they will gather out of His kingdom all stumbling blocks, and those who commit lawlessness,
[42] and will cast them into the furnace of fire; in that place there shall be weeping and gnashing of teeth. (Mat 13:41-42 NAS)

bible. And like our entity, _Echad_ does not need interpretation, translation, or organization[39]. Humans take it as a great insult when we are accused of being something we are not. How do you think God feels when we replace Him with organization and organizational leaders? We can see glimpses of entity in the concept of conscience. One does not need to belong to an organization to have a conscience. Your conscience does not have a list of good and evil, right, and wrong. It knows it innately. It is the source of the claim of people attempting to validate themselves. The claim that "I am a good person". As I wrote in my first book, our conscience is the conduit to our spirit and our spirit is the conduit to the Holy Spirit. It may very well be that conscience is spiritual genetics with receptors originally activated when God walked with Adam and Eve in the Garden of Eden[40]. Conscience is a conduit that was pinched off from knowing God better, blocked by our brokenness, but some connections remained. In the same way arteriosclerosis inhibits proper blood flow to the lungs and heart, so does our brokenness hinder

---

[39] Thus says the LORD, "Heaven is My throne, and the earth is My footstool. Where then is a house you could build for Me? (Isa 66:1 NAS)

[40] And they heard the sound of the LORD God walking in the garden in the cool of the day, (Gen 3:8 NAS)

those conduits of communication to be flowing freely. Unhindered connections with _Echad_ entity do not provide religious data, like organizations. It provides the ability to know the companionship of another being by not existing alone. This is why Jesus sent the Holy Spirit to help each of us. This is _Echad_ relationship, Entity to entity relationship. When properly connected to the Holy Spirit, we spiritually breath with Jesus and The Father. We are _Echad_ with Jesus[41], we are One.

---

[41] So that they all may be one even as You, Father, are in me and I am in You that they also may be in us; (Joh 17:21 MW)

Religion

Recently I was reminded of Karl Marx' quote that "religion was the opiate of the masses"[42]. It was by a nominal Christian who believes that this life is all that exists. There is no afterlife. First, I congratulate this person for their honesty. Many times, people will not even engage with me on the topic of religion, let alone express their final conclusions and opinions. This interaction brought me to consider the many conversations I had over the years with individuals about religion, life, the afterlife, death, etc. In these conversations there exists various opinions about religion but few about contacting God. What I am inferring is: God always seems to be a significant distance from the human being. And often people who claim to hear from God are laughed out of the room. In my first book, He Will Guide You, I make the point that the bible can be manipulated to express many contradictory statements about its content, God, and religion. This is not unusual to me because the bible is not a religious book. It is a book about God relating to

---

[42] https://www.learnreligions.com/karl-marx-on-religion-251019

cultures of humanity, mainly the Jewish culture. It does not espouse a ruling class, it defines relationship, respect, and order. Contrary to Christian theology, it does not establish church offices and titles. Religion has adulterated and manipulated normal words of the past and made them into religious words and present-day dogma. When the bible mentions pastors, evangelists, and prophets, such as in Ephesians chapter four, they were non-religious words depicting the activities of individuals at that time. They were lay terms portraying what people were doing or where they were going. Apostle is a verb, not a noun. It means to be sent. They were sent out to spread the message of the Messiah. Today, religion implies that the title apostle is a title of privilege, it is something beyond a job. It has become a noun. Similarly, if a predicate such as garbage collector was the job in the early church, we might have a church title of garbage man in place of pastor. What I am saying is you cannot make someone into a shepherd (Pastor) of people, it is the natural activity of an individual to concern themselves with people in a certain manner. It does not take a title. It takes a life of action. It takes relational caring and compassion. A perfect example is motherhood. There are many women who perform the duties of motherhood and never had a child of their own. It is a natural bent, a natural process, not an office or religious title. But by religious standards, if motherhood was mentioned in the bible, it would be a church office title today. Too many people have been burned out and walked away from God because they were trying to be a religious "something" they were not created to be and too many adherents were tossed into the dumpster in the same way children are discarded by would-be mothers. Fortunately, like the garbage man, God can rescue us from religion. Religion detracts from and replaces the voice of the Holy Spirit. Religion distorts the concept of faith in God. Religion offers a temporary and false sense of security, exchanging a sacred relationship with The Creator for human-made idol worship.

Pharaoh's Light

The chapter following this one is on judgment. The purpose of this chapter is to assist in understanding why judgment exists. Humanity does not like the word judgment when it is used in reference to God and religion. The reason is many bible proclaiming people, religious people, remind others that judgment is mentioned in the bible and humanity will be judged. While this is accurate, the real aspect that annoys people is the "suffering in hell" part of the warning. Yes, the bible does contain many warnings. One of those warnings has to do with God's sovereignty[43]. God is the Creator, the Ruler, and the best hope we have for avoiding trouble. There are biblical recordings where God's sovereignty seems unfair[44], but that is one of the conundrums connected to the sovereignty principle. Yet, let me assure you that God, while sovereign, is compassionate and merciful. One of the biblical

---

[43] The Son of Man will send forth His angels, and they will gather out of His kingdom all stumbling blocks, and those who commit lawlessness,
and will cast them into the furnace of fire; in that place there shall be weeping and gnashing of teeth. (Mat 13:41-42 NAS)

[44] Then God said to Noah, "The end of all flesh has come before Me; for the earth is filled with violence because of them; and behold, I am about to destroy them with the earth. (Gen 6:13 NAS)

interactions that demonstrates God's sovereignty and compassion is often misunderstood. In the book of Exodus, God tells Moses that He is going to harden the heart of Pharoah against Moses and the Israelites[45]. On the surface it seems unfair because not only can God do what He can do but God does it also. So, the blame falls on God from many people who know the story. Why did God have to harden Pharaoh's heart? Did God take over Pharoah's freewill? Did Pharoah have a choice? If one takes a moment to think through the process, it is not God doing the hardening, it is the Pharaoh's choice. Yet, hardening would not exist unless God established this principle by enabling our free will to reject Him, this is God's sovereignty in motion[46]. God's sovereignty allows us to choose a path. It also establishes good and evil. Pharoah had the same freewill that you and I have, a freewill that God will not override, but when that freewill chooses to challenge God, God's sovereignty directs the result. Pharoah chose to challenge God and he lost. God cannot and does not shy away from Truth, God did harden Pharoah's heart because He is the Creator and

---

[45] But I will harden his heart so that he will not let the people go (Exo 4:21 NAS)
[46] The king's heart is *like* channels of water in the hand of the LORD; He turns it wherever He wishes. (Pro 21:1 NAS)

is responsible for the principle. Similarly, people who hate God is not God's doing, it is simply <u>because of</u> God's doing. What I am saying is God is just being God. In the interaction with Pharoah, Pharoah does not like that God's sovereignty squashed Pharoah's sovereignty. Because of God's response to the challenge, Pharoah's anger is directed toward God's people. The voice of anger overtakes him[47]. But Pharoah was offered "light". In fact, every human is offered "light" from God. And every human is given a choice, like Pharoah[48], and everyone has an opportunity to respond. As I wrote in my last book, when each person stands before The King, their attitude toward this "light" will be the focus. There are people who reject God's light, don't be one of them. God can do nothing other than be God, not because God has any hindrances but because God is Who He is. God is just, merciful, forgiving. Yet, God is unyielding, sovereign, and steadfast in ruling and judging all that

---

[47] The rules of Echad existence are set already. Ignoring God, fighting God, hating God naturally incur results. It is similar to holding your hand over a flame. Doing such will yield a result. It is God's fault? God's plan for His creation is set in motion because of God's Being. God is productive, not destructive. But when humans choose not to embrace God's productiveness, they choose the opposite. People rage against God over this principle because of religion.

[48] "Then you shall say to Pharaoh, 'Thus says the LORD, "Israel is My son, My first-born. [23] "So I said to you, 'Let My son go, that he may serve Me'; but you have refused to let him go. (Exo 4:22-23 NAS)

exists. Every day people get angry with God for many reasons. Their problem is the same a Pharoah's. Here is a list:

1. God let something bad happen.
2. God did not stop something bad from happening.
3. God did not answer me.
4. God did not help me.
5. God waited too long.
6. Why did God let this happen?
7. Why does God let good things happen to bad people?
8. Why does God let bad things happen to good people?

Every day every person's life presents opportunities to walk with God and to accept the guidance from the Holy Spirit. There is this "light" that offers a path of mercy, forgiveness, and compassion towards us and those we encounter. Don't be like Pharoah, don't miss the "light".

Judgment

When one reads the word judgment in a book such as mine, a book listed under the umbrella of faith, the word judgment becomes a religious word. We begin to remember the concepts of religious judgment, and punishments that we do not like to be reminded of, such as eternal suffering, fire, and brimstone. We ultimately bump into the word hell, which has very little use for the general public unless we are referring to a political opponent. But I would like to turn the discussion to a less volatile topic, a much easier tone to digest mentally, and emotionally. I want to speak about the word opinion. We all use the word opinion when we attach it to a softer judgment. People will throw up their hands and say, it is only my opinion.

We all have an opinion. For myself, I have attempted to mute the idea of opinion, unless absolutely pressed, because it has a frequent companion known as emotion. We can refer to this combination of emotion and judgment as a strong opinion. Due to emotion, I find, in many cases, that opinion is as far away from the voice of the Holy Spirit as one can get. This is because emotion is easily manipulated by the voice of the demonic. My journey with the Holy Spirit grew as I began to "hear" the words that came from my mouth and the mouths of others and realized the Holy Spirit was not the voice behind them. Consider this list of opinions:

1. I hate that football team!
2. I hate that quarterback!
3. I hate that coach!
4. She annoys me every time she opens her mouth!
5. Those parents don't know how to raise a child!
6. Look at the car he drives, show-off!
7. This politician is clueless!
8. I hope they die.
9. I would like to see that politician go to jail!
10. I do not believe in another life; this is the end!
11. Go to hell!
12. I do not trust these people!
13. That talk show host makes me sick every time they open their mouth!
14. My neighbor is always making too much noise in their yard!
15. I cannot believe that idiot in the other car just cut me off!

16. If that politician gets elected, they will ruin the country!

These opinions (judgments) determine who we are as a human. I am aware you don't like what I just said. I know it makes you uncomfortable. And, true to my writing, what you think about those statements is ultimately between you and the Holy Spirit for final conviction. But, if we cannot hear ourselves, we cannot change ourselves. And if we cannot hear God, we cannot follow the Holy Spirit's suggestions[49] because true obedience can only occur after recognition. Broken humans cannot tolerate humanity, especially when humanity has a different opinion. The annoyance can be a parent, spouse, child, neighbor, stranger, and sometimes even themselves! We are full of judgment, sorry I meant to say opinion. We are overrun by opinion. Most of my reference so far has been to "noisy" opinion. But we are also overrun by the silent opinion of self, the world and the demonic. It is like a television series running episode after episode in our minds. We cannot turn it off. The reason is that it is linked to the anger we

---

[49] And the angel of the LORD appeared to him in a blazing fire from the midst of a bush; and he looked, and behold, the bush was burning with fire, yet the bush was not consumed (Exo 3:2 NAS)

humans hold beneath the surface. The reruns of an alone mind invaded by the angry voice of the demonic are why we cannot sleep, why we overeat, why we are on antidepressants, and why we are just unhappy.

If you have not figured it out at this point, broken humanity is filled with anger, and it is usually expressed in opinion. Anger is unseen so we can suppress it, ignore it, and deny it. We have ourselves convinced it is not relevant due to the ebb and tide of the process. Yet, we know it exists because it rears its ugly head at times and in sober human moments we are convicted. It is an internal moment. It is a quiet moment. It is a conscience moment. It is a real moment. It is a moment of truth. We don't admit to it because it reveals our ugliness. We know ugly. We can recognize ugly. We see it every day on the news. We don't like ugly, especially when we see it in ourselves. So, we say:

1. I was only joking.
2. I don't really hate that player.
3. It is only a figure of speech.
4. It was only a momentary lapse of control.
5. I am only concerned because of what the world will become for my grandchildren.

We attempt to soften it, dress it up and put a bow on it, but we know in our knower it is human ugliness, encouraged by the voices of the demonic and of the world. Human opinion acts out its daily routine by blocking the voice of the Holy Spirit. Human opinion, which is angry with God, the God who reaches out every day in compassion and mercy to each human.

I was recently speaking to someone who did not like my word brokenness. They thought it was too harsh. They preferred the word imperfect. My initial comment was acceptance of the word as a substitute. They did not necessarily see the equivalency. After some consideration, I have formed an opinion, a judgment, on the exchange and the word. The word imperfect is less ugly than the word broken. It is less judgmental. It presents a condition more repairable than broken. It presents a condition for which we are less responsible. Imperfect offers the illusion of attaining perfection, broken cannot because even when we fix something that was broken, we will always be cognizant of the fact it was broken. Imperfection is simply another opinion. It is simply another judgment emanating from broken humanity, just not so ugly.

The voice of the Holy Spirit teaches the individual personal and personally relevant guard rails to establish for one's life. By receiving and recognizing the voice of the Holy Spirit, one can stay ahead of the challenges and inclinations to run off at the mouth without considering one's personal life, actions, and opinions. In other words, the broken individuals that comprise humanity, a humanity filled with hypocrisy, can be less hypocritical. Now there is an opinion! What is the benefit? You can walk with God and embrace the completeness that can grow with that relationship. A relationship that recognizes, judges, and cuts off the voices of the demonic and the world at every intersection.

Power Over the Mind

We live in a political world. You may not agree but every topic has been politicized. The most common are gender, abortion, gun violence, and healthcare. While the pandemic made healthcare politicization obvious, for decades drug companies have bought politicians to promote treatments that have made them second to none in wealth. As I like to put it, drug companies have "deep pockets". Sports have been confiscated by athletes more focused on what they say, wear and where they go rather than being successful at their profession. Successful and powerful business executives, for centuries, have sought political office because of the power it represents. Money is a huge advantage in politics. With the advent of mass media, many individuals, politicians included, have signed contracts with huge media companies to create programs, television series and movies to promote their philosophy. Being president of the United States was the ultimate power. This is not true any longer. Having a media-based program broadcast now across the entire globe is the new power. Children (for example college students) are signing multi-million-dollar contracts as "influencers". The core issue here is the ability to influence thought, which can influence actions because it influences people. The mind is where power really has its effect. Movies that have portrayed the lifestyles of people in organized crime demonstrate the extent power affects the human being's mind. The participants kill others in pursuit of their goals. And then we see movies about the law-abiding government organizations prosecuting organized crime groups. The irony of it all is there is little difference between the driving force of both law enforcement and criminals. This force is the desire for the power that can change a person's mind through fear and punishment! And as you have heard before, power corrupts.

Power over the mind has long been desired by humans. It was first desired by Satan, who instigated Eve to desire the same. She coerced the silent Adam[50]. God, who is the only one with real power, endowed humanity with a freewill, the source of power. But in this realm power is confined to the mind and can only be unleashed on an individual basis through physical

---

[50] Then to Adam He (God) said, "Because you have listened to the voice of your wife, and have eaten from the tree about which I commanded you, saying, 'You shall not eat from it';..... (Gen 3:17 NAS)

action. If you don't believe me, think about the power Jesus demonstrated[51]. Freewill, the ability to choose, while being the greatest gift from God, has become the weakest link of humanity. Why? It is like possessing a gun. Guns are objects that can destroy life, so can a hammer. But unlike a hammer, a gun can unintentionally do damage. When the power of freewill is mishandled or ignored, it can do damage. It began with Adam and Eve and is evidenced throughout the violent history of humanity. Every hour of every day human minds are unleashing hate and anger with words and actions.

Since the Garden of Eden, humanity has had a major problem, it is called death. Death cannot be avoided, obliterated, or bought off. It overcame humanity like a gun going off in the wrong direction[52]. No amount of human design can fix the result of Adam's bad choice, so death ends our trial of possessing human power. Humanity, since it cannot fix the result of death, throughout the ages has focused on the second-best

---

[51] And when He had said these things, He cried out with a loud voice, "Lazarus, come forth." 44 He who had died came forth (Joh 11:43-44 NAS)

[52] "From any tree of the garden you may eat freely; 17 but from the tree of the knowledge of good and evil you shall not eat, for in the day that you eat from it you shall surely die." (Gen 2:16-17 NAS)

option, human thought. Controlling other humans offers the controller the mental high of power through direction of the minds of others. If you are not convinced, try eliminating the media from your life. It, like all social media, is an addiction. Religion has its share of mind-controlling seekers. Jim Jones murdered his followers when they voluntarily drank the poisoned juice. Story after story of individuals escaping religious cults has been told.

God, on the other hand, does not operate in this manner. If you do not deny the existence of God, then you may agree God has power. Yet, God does not exert that power over humanity. God gave us freewill to choose a value system, God's system, or Satan's' system. Let us look at the enemy we face.

Deception

The best way to get someone to do something stupid is to frame it in a way in which it does not seem stupid. I watched a movie last week. It was about exorcism. I never watch horror movies, but the religious implications piqued my curiosity. So, I watched the movie because I needed to confirm that the demonic realm was continuing to maintain deceptiveness concerning humanity's idea of demonic spirits. It is a stupid deception veiled in religious ideology and, unfortunately, people believe what they are offered. I very much believe in another realm. I very much believe in the demonic. What I do not believe in is Hollywood and its portrayal of the demonic. Two prominent voices, the demonic and the world, combined with the silence of self, make a tripod stool on which many people and many media companies sit. These are the cheap seats ushered in by Adam and Eve. From those cheap seats, they conceive movies that are framed by an opinion, not reality. The concepts are stupid.

I need to be very clear in explaining this situation. Evil exists and can be both explained and demonstrated by an array of magnitude, a scale. Let me elaborate on this scale of demonic activity in which humans participate. Yes, evil is demonstrated by wanton acts of cruelty, brutality, and malice perpetrated not by unseen spirits but by humans. While being the far end of the scale, we are duped, by movies, to believe this is the gateway, the full spectrum of demonic activity. It is not. The middle of the scale is a display of evil which presents itself as what many would consider "normal" behavior. The normal behavior of anger, envy, deception, frustration, and lack of compassion, while being the mid-range of the scale, is still very serious demonic influence. This is the fog in which the daily activities of humanity take place. The other end of this scale is the most deceptive, it is the angel of light[53] activity. As the bible puts it, this is the wolf in sheep's clothing phenomenon[54]. It is constant fraudulent religious activity. This deceit begins in the mind of the human, and it is released into actions by human cooperation. History has a clear record of events such as the crusades, but it is the ongoing unrecognized

---

[53] And no wonder, for Satan himself masquerades as an angel of light. (2Co 11:14 NIV)

[54] 15 "Beware of the false prophets, who come to you in sheep's clothing, but inwardly are ravenous wolves. 16 "You will know them by their fruits. Grapes are not gathered from thorn *bushes*, nor figs from thistles, are they? (Mat 7:15-16 NAS)

religious activity overseen by this "angel of light" that is most deceptive.

What is the extent of demonic activity on an individual? Humanity can be inflicted with depression, oppression, and possession. Demonic spirits do have the ability to possess a human being, but only with that individual's acquiesce. These individuals may injure themselves, such as cutting themselves with a knife[55]. The movie I watched, deceptively, made it appear that the demon was causing physical damage such as knife cuts. This cannot occur without assistance from the individual. This next sentence is very important. The demonic spirit does not have the ability to produce an injury, for example, a cut with a knife or a moving lump in the skin or a broken bone from inside of the body. The injury must be self-inflicted. To counter my point some will cite the book of Job. In the book of Job, God removed His protection from Job, but it was other humans and nature[56] who did the damage, not spirits from the next realm. Additionally, it was only after God

---

[55] So they shouted louder and slashed themselves with swords and spears, as was their custom, until their blood flowed. (1Ki 18:28 NIV)

[56] While he was still speaking, another messenger came and said, "The Chaldeans formed three raiding parties and swept down on your camels and made off with them. They put the servants to the sword, and I am the only one who has escaped to tell you!"

removed this protection that allowed disease, skin boils, to afflict Job but keep in mind, Job was never possessed, just attacked with physical sickness. This is very different than what exorcism movies present. The demonic uses an array of tools to deceive people. The silence of the voice of self, combined with the deceptive voices of the demonic and the world led humans to a place where the voice of the Holy Spirit is drowned out. This has invited human trouble[57].

There is another scale that applies to human psychological troubles. The evil of demonic possession exists on one end of this scale. Depression and oppression, conditions closer to the center of the meter are much more prevalent in society. The far end of this scale is represented by the zealous behavior of functional political, religious, and social groups masquerading as normal but proliferating anger, frustration and hate towards those who disagree with them.

---

[57] From any tree of the garden you may eat freely; [17] but from the tree of the knowledge of good and evil you shall not eat, for in the day that you eat from it you shall surely die." (Gen 2:16-17 NAS)

It is my belief as a medical professional that most of humanity affected by these multitudes of demonic attacks would rather not have them occur, but I could be wrong. Recognition of the voices is the first and biggest step in the battle. Humanity can deny access to the demonic if they can recognize the attack. They would resist the underlying anger that exists inside. They would recognize the voice of the Holy Spirit which would put a spotlight on this other activity. The problem is deception. Many people simply do not believe what I am saying. Why? They claim the bible is not compatible with science. The bible is not relevant to these issues. The bible is too narrow in the data. The bible is too old, and the information is outdated. These are physical diseases that only prescription medication can help. And ultimately, God does not exist.

I have seen humanity struggle with its aloneness. I have dispensed antidepressant after antidepressant while people fight for their lives, their minds, and their existence. They are also fighting for their family, friends, and some, for humanity itself. The battle is hard, and victory can only be found in learning to hear and obey the voice of the Holy Spirit. This Comforter desires a personal relationship with everyone. The Holy Spirit is not represented by religion or religious people. There is no organization representing the Holy Spirit. People think the bible is a religious book. It is not. It is a relationship book demonstrating relational existence with God, or without. The voice of the Holy Spirit can reach within each person. Each of us must make a foundational decision. Do we listen, believe, and obey the deceptive voices of the demonic and the world or, do we listen to and believe the voice of the Holy Spirit. The first step is to believe the Holy Spirit exists[58]! The Holy Spirit exposes deception and can help you see more clearly.

---

[58] And without faith it is impossible to please God, because anyone who comes to him must believe that he exists and that he rewards those who earnestly seek him. (Heb 11:6 NIV)

The Paradox of Humanity

We are born into a temporal reality. It is temporary. For most of us, it begins well. We are fed and provided for until that time whereby we must provide for ourselves. This temporal reality also has some challenges for us. There is aging, sickness, and death. Humanity has also come up with some positives, mostly because God said we could.[59] We are free to experience notoriety, fame, religion, politics, finance, academia, knowledge, data, materials, nature and more. All of these offer us the opportunity to excel in this existence. To become comfortable. To live freely. Many people would agree they are free, they would just like to be freer. Yes, we have some obligations to the government but, as long as we pay, we can remain free.

The opposite of freedom is not captivity. The opposite of freedom is deception. This is the reason we seek to be freer, such as libertarians. They do not want to be shackled with government taxes, government expenses and government waste, in other words, someone else's brokenness. To some extent the

---

[59] The LORD said, "If as one people speaking the same language they have begun to do this, then nothing they plan to do will be impossible for them. (Gen 11:6 NIV)

libertarian is not deceived by politics but they, like all, are in bondage. The deception of being free obscures the spiritual state of humanity and the ignorance attached to daily life. The bible says Jesus set the captives free[60]. Jesus said we were in bondage[61]. Jesus himself said he came to bring freedom. Which is correct? Humanity exists in a deceptive paradox. We live in a real world and a pretend world at the same time. In some Hollywood movies people are made to believe they are free through some sort of mental deception. The mind is tricked to believe something exists that does not exist. One famous movie has people living in a computer program while their unconscious body was hard wired into the program. We are not in a movie, but we are in a deceptive existence. During the movie, the pinnacle of human brokenness is personified when one of the characters in the movie chooses a made-up existence as opposed to a harsh reality of real life. Humanity is not far from this behavior. On one end of the scale, we live in a world where we are deceived to believe hate, anger,

---

[60] "The Spirit of the Lord is upon Me, Because He anointed Me to preach the gospel to the poor. He has sent Me to proclaim release to the captives, (Luk 4:18 NAS)

[61] Jesus answered them, "Truly, truly, I say to you, everyone who commits sin is the slave of sin. 35 "And the slave does not remain in the house forever; the son does remain forever. 36 "If therefore the Son shall make you free, you shall be free indeed. (Joh 8:34-36 NAS)

frustration, violence, and such are acceptable in certain circumstances. On the other end, the deeper ruse is we distance ourselves from the ugliness. We ignore, or worse yet deny, that we are participants in this ugliness. We are deceived to think that manipulative rationale, and sometimes even non-violent vengeance, is warranted decision-making. The non-violent litigious manipulations of society, at times, have done more damage than the violent side. This causes us to rationalize that we are good more than we are bad, as if that makes bad excusable. And we do it all never taking the time to delineate what exactly bad means. We don't delineate because we believe that opinion is fact. We believe movies, deceptive ones, express truth. They suggest demonic activity only exists on the evilest end of the meter and in the end, the demonic is overcome, which leads to freedom. The lack of recognition of evil does not lead to freedom, it leads to deception which causes human bondage. This bondage to notoriety, fame, religion, politics, finance, academia, knowledge, data, material, wealth, and nature exists everywhere. I am not against social fixes, but we accomplish them at the expense of compassion, mercy, and kindness, which is no accomplishment at all[62].

We are deceived by human made laws which are manipulated by those in charge to instill fear in others. This keeps humanity not in a Hollywood-made computer program but in a real-world milieu of human and demonic deception, a world where the longing to be free emanates from the spirit we don't even know exists. Humanity misses it because freedom does not begin in the flesh, it begins in the mind, even in the spirit.

That spirit can be communicated with, even touched, by the Holy Spirit, whether that touch is sentient, aware, or naïve of the source. The voice of the Holy Spirit guides us to put others first, teaches self-denial, self-forgiveness, self-judgment, and orchestrates a symphony of compassion that, over time, consumes them. They do not become perfect people, they just recognize deception and understand that forgiveness, mercy, and compassion lead to freedom. I am not perfect. I make bad and wrong decisions at times. I cannot fix my brokenness one hundred percent, but I can work on myself project by project, hearing the voice

---

[62] For all of us have become like one who is unclean, And all our righteous deeds are like a filthy garment; (Isa 64:6 NAS)

of the Holy Spirit reminding me of what I have learned. I will have many decisions to account for when I stand before the King but, none of them have the power to steal my freedom in Jesus. My journey to the next realm, like yours, is filled with potholes of hate, anger, unforgiveness, hurt and more but the Holy Spirit journeys with me, right next to me helping me recognize the terrain. The Holy Spirit, like a road crew, works on filling in some of these potholes keeping me from crashes instigated by the distracting voices of the world and the demonic. For a long time, I have known what is required of me[63]. And every day I am made aware of any new requirements. I don't mind them because when I stand before the King, I will be able to say, "I have done what was required of me, Lord". I desire no title, reward or pat on the back. Being with the King will be enough. God is my reward.

Let me share a story with you, a schoolboy story, a story that I only remember because of the voice of the Holy Spirit. When I was in eighth grade, I challenged the priest at the school I attended concerning the next life. We were discussing death and he said, "when you die

---

[63] "So you too, when you do all the things which are commanded you, say, 'We are unworthy slaves; we have done *only* that which was required of us.'" (Luk 17:10 NAS)

you see the face of Jesus for eternity". I thought that was creepy. Laying in a coffin, not being able to move, looking at someone's face, forever. He was a nice guy, but he did not do such a great job explaining it. God did years later. It was not so much an explanation as it was a revelation. In my two previous books I spoke extensively about The King, my King, Jesus. And my King is more than enough to spend eternity with and in him I will find The Father. The Father will lead me to all joy not only to see and be with Himself, but with all those who love Him. Those will be the people I long to see and be with, people I knew and did not know. People who embraced the cognition of hearing God's Voice and who were obedient to that Voice. This is what the priest did not elaborate on, but that is okay. God finished the job to setting me free spiritually. Don't accept the paradox of humanity. Let the voice of the Holy Spirit guide you daily in freedom, in compassion, in mercy, in kindness, and forgiveness. Desire to see the source of those truths and leave the paradox behind.

The Problem with Doctrine

I wanted to deal with religious doctrine and the effects of its creation by religious organizations. A few centuries ago, the Monk Martin Luther posted ninety-five theses, or statements, contradicting religious doctrine. One of these was related to the existence of a place known as purgatory and the subsequent retention or release of the individuals being held in this place post-death. Their release was dependent on how much money their living relatives placed on the offering plate. I don't know if people still believe in purgatory, but the doctrine was absurd on its face and contradictory to biblical content. The next realm does exist and is as good a place as any to start when considering religious doctrine. But you may be skeptical. You may ask, "does the next realm exist?" If so, what are the possible environments? What is the status of those who get to this realm? Is it comfortable? Is it painful? What is a day like? Do the actions of this life determine the environment of that existence? Some religious individuals I speak to claim that there is universal salvation. This is a belief that everyone will face a comfortable eternal existence in the next realm. Religious organizations pose different particulars concerning this topic. The marketing details each organization has set in place as doctrine concerning the next realm are meant to ease fear because departing this life can cause much fear. Most of the talk surrounding universal salvation is about going to heaven. Which heaven one goes to is the real question. Some of the next life doctrines are focused on living on the earth in a similar fashion to our current existence. Religious doctrines are like vacations spots. Some people like Europe, others like the Islands, still others like their backyard. You can pick your organization by its doctrine. As both of my last two writings explain, the transition to the next realm and the "meet" with The King will manage all confusion. This is why it is so vital that you make the attempt to hear, and follow, the voice of the Holy Spirit while in this realm. The Holy Spirit represents the King. The Holy Spirit leads us to the King, religious doctrine does not. The bible states that, eventually, humans will live on the new earth[64]. It speaks of garden-like environment[65]

---

[64] And I saw a new heaven and a new earth; for the first heaven and the first earth passed away, and there is no longer *any* sea. (Rev 21:1 NAS)

[65] And he showed me a river of the water of life, clear as crystal, coming from the throne of God and of the Lamb, 2 in the middle of its street. And on either side of the river was the tree of life, bearing twelve *kinds of* fruit, yielding its fruit every month; and the leaves of the tree were for the healing of the nations. (Rev 22:1-2 NAS)

but most important The Father and The Son will be the focal point providing the light in which raised from the dead eternal human beings[66] will exist with their God. The bible also states that not all humans will experience this eternity. That said, you don't need the bible to realize the state of humanity belies the possibility of universal salvation, or universal eternal existence without some significant transformation in the human attitude. The doctrine of universal salvation is a practical conundrum in our present condition. Humanity lacks the compassion, mercy, and patience[67] needed to exist with each other in peace forever. It is also an option that the bible seems to flatly contradict[68][69]. Let's examine the topic.

---

[66] For the Lord Himself will descend from heaven with a shout, with the voice of *the* archangel, and with the trumpet of God; and the dead in Messiah shall rise first. (1Th 4:16 NAS)

[67] But the fruit of the Spirit is love, joy, peace, patience, kindness, goodness, faithfulness, [23] gentleness, self-control; against such things there is no law. (Gal 5:22-23 NAS)

[68] Enter by the narrow gate; for the gate is wide, and the way is broad that leads to destruction, and many are those who enter by it. [14] "For the gate is small, and the way is narrow that leads to life, and few are those who find it. (Mat 7:13-14 NAS)

[69] Jesus said to him, "I am the way, and the truth, and the life; no one comes to the Father, but through Me. (Joh 14:6 NAS)

Universal Salvation

Universal salvation is a great idea on its face. We have little need to talk about judgment, sin, brokenness, imperfection or even God. Everyone will make it to the next realm and all will be hunky dory. But a quick look around at the world and there are some serious questions to ask. Humans hate one another. If you don't agree just turn on the television. Social media also reveals the anger of humanity. The political arena is a good example of human brokenness. We humans not only have trouble agreeing on political topics but, there is the literal expression of the hate I just mentioned. And in many cases, it is cloaked in niceness, calmness, and civility, until it isn't. How can we reconcile hating for eternity? Consider divorce; It is necessary for some people to get divorced because they cannot exist in the same house together. How will people exist in the same place for eternity hating one another? Maybe hate is too strong for you. How about a simple difference of opinion. I have sat at a table with family members who have a different opinion than I do on various topics. They can barely keep their seat, and ultimately, don't. They may not claim to hate me, but they surely have difficulty tolerating me. There are many hot button topics such as race, gender, abortion, same sex unions, environment, etc. So, the idea of humanity simply transferring to the next realm in the same state as we exist in this realm is challenging, and maybe even disturbing.

The Concept of Obedience

The universality of the concept of obedience is rarely realized. I liken it to the concept of the universality of trust. Humanity enacts trust, and obedience, without even a thought. When we want something, and we often do, we usually will take whatever steps of obedience, discipline and compliance are required to attain that desire. One example is buying a house. There are many tedious steps to the process. Most new home buyers acquiesce because they want the house. Another example is Christmas. Many anticipate it with excitement. Christmas is a favorite for many people, including many non-Christians. I have seen plenty of Jewish, Hindu, and Muslim individuals participate in the Christmas gift giving process. They want to be part of, included in and involved with their friends who participate in the ritual. To do this one must embrace obedience to the process even when not necessarily agreeing with the religious meaning of the holiday, and people do it. Obedience is seen, if one wishes to be legal and successful, in all the following:

1. Paying taxes
2. Driving a motor vehicle

3. Attending a school

4. Working a job

5. Being part of

    a. A Marriage

    b. A Religion

    c. Politics

6. Profession such as

    a. Pharmacist

    b. Lawyer

    c. Doctor

Obedience comes in the form of following the proper philosophical, emotional, and scientific standards established to be successful. But our attention to the idea of obedience is often obscured by our desire to attain the goal. We just don't realize we are being obedient.

The Results of Obedience

Obedience does not exist naturally. If one seeks to be obedient in any task, they usually are required to go through a series of steps or procedures. This is known as discipline. Learning to be part of a culture or religion requires obedience, discipline, and compliance. Earning a college or postgraduate degree is another good example. Individuals who earn such degrees have been responsible for many important tasks such as building a skyscraper, delivering a baby, designing a plane and much more. As we grow older, we better appreciate the value of the discipline of obedience because we see its level of pervasiveness in human success. And allow me to digress for one moment. If one is really perceptive, they can see God's effect through human success. Now back to the topic. Additionally, realizing that we participate in this process voluntarily has much value. It exposes freewill and the freedom of choice. It reveals the depth of humankind. It can also make us feel better about ourselves. These are some of the results of being obedient. There is one important truth to keep in mind. Since obedience originates with God, much of the process that I describe about humankind can include hearing the truth of the Holy Spirit. God exists and permeates society in all the good that humankind has and will accomplish. This is an outward work of God and different than the indwelling of the Holy Spirit.

Discipline Compliance Obedience

When the employee I mentioned earlier commented that the propositions in my writings were "hard to do", I realized that cognition must precede obedience. I pointed out to her that she heard the voice of the Holy Spirit due to the sense of conviction she felt. She became cognizant of the truth. She could not just ignore the experience. There is quite a bit of information we encounter daily. Understanding what comes from God can make us obedient to God. Religion cannot provide internal conviction, only external reactions such as embarrassment, regret, pity, or anger. When these feelings happen, the frustration for getting caught is a thought often instigated by the demonic. The voice of the Holy Spirit is different than religion. Because you are experiencing truth, obedience requires discipline and compliance. This is the chain reaction my employee experienced. You experience it as your personal requirement but are unsure how to proceed, just like my employee. Thus, like our regular daily activities where process is necessary to be obedient to something or someone, a journey with the Holy Spirit requires the same discipline, compliance, and obedience. Discipline is the effort required to complete a task. Compliance is completing it correctly. I own a home. Our town provides services. Three of those services are garbage, cardboard, and comingled collection. I must have the discipline to place the required item at my curb for the pickup to occur. If I don't, I will be overrun with each waste item. I must also be compliant to place the correct item at the curb at the correct time. As a pharmacist, it is vital that I dispense every prescription correctly. My staff and I had to develop procedures for checking and double-checking our work. And it takes discipline and compliance to adhere to these processes even though they are repetitive, simple, and mundane. Years ago, I took up jogging. It is probably the one practice in my life that developed the discipline which has become routine for all I do, especially the aspect of my relationship with the Holy Spirit. At one point I was jogging thirty miles a week. It was those miles that provided the opportunity to hear the Holy Spirit. It was those miles where cognition finally occurred. In the discipline of jogging and the cognition of hearing, the Holy Spirit presented me with the natural next step for my humanity, the option of compliance.

Unless the three legs of discipline, compliance and obedience exist spiritually, the stool of hearing the Holy Spirit cannot be built. This is a seat that takes us out of the cheap seats that humanity occupies due to Adam and Eve. This seat is front and center to the voice of the Holy Spirit. This seat is front and center to the correct Jesus. And this is not a seat of judgment. This is a seat of learning, instruction, and growth. It is a place of relationship, discussion, questions, answers, compassion, mercy, and hope[70]. It is also a place of challenge, correction, and truth. And most importantly, it is a place of freedom, freedom to stay seated or freedom to get up and walk away. The option is obedience to The Voice or rejection of The Voice. Unlike religion, obedience does not mean salvation and rejection does not mean damnation. Unlike religion, the Holy Spirit requires no money. Unlike religion the Holy Spirit does not take attendance. In a real sense our relationship with God is somewhat al a cart because brokenness in this life can never morph to perfection. But we can develop a discipline to make sure we are removing the garbage on schedule. That compliance

---

[70] 'For I know the plans that I have for you,' declares the LORD, 'plans for welfare and not for calamity to give you a future and a hope. (Jer 29:11 NAS)

leads to greater obedience as we recognize the voice to follow, the voice of the Holy Spirit.

Want

Human want exists, and it is different from passion. It is the direct opponent of obedience, discipline, and compliance. We live in broken human vessels that have weaknesses. Jesus knows this fact[71]. There are times in my life when fatigue catches up with me. There is physical fatigue. And then there is non-physical fatigue, including spiritual, psychological, and emotional fatigue. Physical fatigue usually requires sleep. When non-physical fatigue occurs, we need distraction. So, we play on our phone, watch television, read a book, etc. Social media is the breeding ground for distraction. Hunger is another type of example. We need to eat but we can also want to eat. I like chocolate ganache cake. I never "need" to eat chocolate ganache cake, it is all about want.

Why is want the opponent to our existence? Because when we succumb to it, it steals our peace. There are several reasons why but let's first examine the "what' of want. The following is a list of wants that often create trouble for humans. The want for:

---

[71] For we do not have a high priest who cannot sympathize with our weaknesses, but One who has been tempted in all things as *we are, yet* without sin. (Heb 4:15 NAS)

1. Power

2. Money

3. Influence

4. Sex

5. Physical satisfaction

Open the news page on your computer and you will see article after article on these topics and the damage they cause to humanity. Want begins in the unseen depths of the mind and its fomented rise drives the body in a certain direction, a wanted direction. Over the years this very serious battle has played out in the media in a comical interaction. We see a person with an angel on one shoulder and the devil on the other vying for control. But they cannot get control unless the subject makes the decision to act. The loser usually disappears in a puff of smoke. This is what occurs in the mind of every human being. Four voices laying down thought. One of those voices, the demonic, doing all in its power to direct human choices and actions. It is generally accompanied by the voice of the world employing worldly data and info to substantiate rationale. The voice of self, usually silent, is attempting to follow the conscience in making better decisions but is hesitant to take a stand without the mob, the voice of the world, on its side. And the voice of the Holy Spirit attempts to rise above even the conscience to provide godly guidance.

This battle is for the ground known as want because want produces actions. Ultimately, the Holy Spirit wants humans to use the free-will which God gave them for godly purposes. Here is a list found in the book of Galatians:

1. Love
2. Joy
3. Peace
4. Patience
5. Kindness
6. Gentleness
7. Goodness
8. Self-Control

Transitioning of want to these attitudes can be long and arduous. It will take discipline, compliance, and obedience. There is no judgment against these actions when they become part of the individual. They cannot cause guilt when the aloneness of the human agrees to the companionship of Jesus through the Holy Spirit and joins in unity with the Creator. Then when one stands before the King someday, they will be commended. With guidance of the indwelling Holy Spirit, freewill controls and directs human desire down the correct path, the path of eternal security.

Eternal Security

What exactly is eternal security and is it attainable? As you can imagine I attempt to speak to people about their faith as often as they engage with me on the topic. A fair number of individuals, usually evangelical Christians, will readily jump into the conversation on various topics, such as salvation, with data and theology they heard proclaimed by sources such as Pastors, books, TV, radio, pod casts and more. Many have been conditioned to reveal what they are taught in the hope of bringing someone to biblical salvation. Salvation is received, biblically, by receiving Jesus as Lord and Savior. But the confines of religion have obscured this biblical truth because receiving internal companionship with the Holy Spirit is different that receiving a relationship with an organization. So, what does this salvation really mean? Let me offer a short history lesson on the origins of the concept of true deliverance. The Jewish word for deliverance is _Yeshua,_ which is also the name Jesus. It is spoken early in the bible by Jacob[72]. Jacob longs to see God's deliverance.

---

[72] (Jacob said) "For Thy deliverance (_yeshua_) I wait, O LORD. (Gen 49:18 NAS)

This _yeshua_ word is recorded hundreds of times in the Tanakh (Old Testament). For the purpose of my writing, the next, most significant, mention of this word is found in Matthew[73]. Joseph, the stepfather of Jesus, is told to name him _Yeshua_ because he will deliver his people from their sins. Jesus, literally, is our deliverance. This verse encompasses the idea of eternal security. Although death will be eventually overcome completely, we are never told we will be saved from death, just from our sins. Sin is what separates humanity from God. Sin is a lack of obedience, compliance, and discipline to God. So, by God's standards, while murder is sin, so is gossip. Eternal security and sin are not compatible. God had to do something about the separation, so The Father sent _Yeshua_.

Salvation, or some sort of eternal existence, is the carrot on the stick of both the church and non-Christian religions, the only difference being that Jesus is not the focal point of other religions. My last two books speak extensively on this topic. In Evangelical Christian theology there is the moment of receiving this

---

[73] behold, an angel of the Lord appeared to him in a dream, saying, "Joseph, son of David, do not be afraid to take Mary as your wife; for that which has been conceived in her is of the Holy Spirit. 21 "And she will bear a Son; and you shall call His name Jesus (_Yeshua_), for it is He who will deliver (_yeshua_) His people from their sins." (Mat 1:20-21 NAS)

promised deliverance. The problem is it is followed by the rest of the organizational process. Bringing new adherents into the church is a common step. The goal of this part of the process is to bring them under the larger organizational umbrella. Church organizational structures listing jobs and titles are common. Allowing people to hear from the Holy Spirit themselves is not promoted by religious organizations yet, this is the real process of deliverance. I, to date, have not found a religious leader who will agree with me concerning the extent of allowing an individual to hear for themselves. How do I know this? Because these leaders would be releasing people from the organization. Yet, they contend people must be walked into the tenets of belief. The problem created is substantial. It translates that the deliverance step is a move in the right direction but there is more to the process. Religious classes, which come next, is where the organization offers the data and knowledge about what God wants from them and, the promises of what God has to offer in return for their acquiescence.

There is also a slew of biblical blessings that they choose to encourage, and entice, the young believer or new member. As people learn about the organization they are brought in deeper. This includes the titles, offices, and ministry appointments as leaders. And don't forget the tithing. There is also a certain prestige that accompanies these titles, though rarely will people acknowledge this fact. Words such as service and calling are rationales that have become commonplace in organizations as a veil used in disguising the sin of human pride. Yet, in the churchgoer there appear levels of dissatisfaction or disgruntlement. This is why church hopping exists. Organizations burn out people who are longing for a relationship with God. To be sure, when you invite Jesus into your being and begin to hear the voice of the indwelling Holy Spirit there exists a process but, unlike religion, it is a personal process concerning one's personal life with advice and direction that cannot be provided corporately. It must be, and is, provided individually. Services and classes cannot replace a daily companion working with you through all you do. This is the experience that leads to eternal security.

Eternal Security is a concept long desired by humanity but what they get is temporal earthly distraction. Don't get me wrong. God is not absent in the process of the life of the individual. With or without religion or church the Holy Spirit is still involved in the life of the individual. God cares for and continues to nurture and intervene, only being limited by organization philosophy and the other voices. Paul said the indwelling presence of the Holy Spirit was our deposit for eternal security[74]. The Pentecostal arm of the church says speaking in tongues is the evidence. The bible makes clear the evidence[75]. A selfless life of love leading to mercy, compassion, and forgiveness. Eternal security can only be experienced with the indwelling Holy Spirit.

---

[74] In Him, you also, after listening to the message of truth, the gospel of your salvation-- having also believed, you were sealed in Him with the Holy Spirit of promise, (Eph 1:13 NAS)

[75] Corinthians Chapter 13

Eternal Life, Attitude, Death

So, what exactly have we been delivered from? We don't like the idea, process, and fact of human death. To demonstrate my point, humans are consumed with the search for eternal life. Movies such as Indiana Jones and The Holy Grail and myths like the Fountain of Youth have occupied humanity for millennia. Biblically, reaching the heavens, not the sky, dates to the Tower of Babel. While some don't believe in another realm, there are those who do seek all the information that is available on that place. There are also people, known as mediums, who speak to spirits. They claim these spirits are deceased relatives of their customers. Each major religion also has its next realm. And then some suggest the idea of returning here to this place as someone or something else. The philosophy is known as reincarnation. But how much can we know and who really knows the truth.

Belief and faith are words that exist in our mind, but we have little to no cognitive understanding of them. Cognition is about how the mind receives, evaluates, and makes conclusions. Human senses are intricately involved in this process. The senses transfer reality to the mind. The problem with the eternal realm is our senses cannot relay the data to our mind. When we cross a bridge successfully for the first time, our physical world and the mind form a link. It is called cognition. We learn trust, faith, and belief. Cognition then allows us to cross any bridge that seems sturdy enough to support us.

But what of that which is beyond our senses? Are there links that can be formed to the invisible, ethereal, spiritual? Religion has attempted to do this for millennia. Religious organizations use data that is related to the spiritual realm reaching into the natural realm[76]. The Judeo-Christian bible is the source for some of this spiritual instruction. People follow religious leaders because they believe that a leader has the necessary connection. But religion has clouded the bible and it purpose. It is like a Christmas tree. There are so many ornaments attached that you lose sight of the tree. So let us strip it down and look to see if we can view what God has offered humanity concerning eternal security.

---

[76] And he had a dream, and behold, a ladder was set on the earth with its top reaching to heaven; and behold, the angels of God were ascending and descending on it. (Gen 28:12 NAS)

If we observe carefully, there is a process that addresses human want. It is called marketing. Marketing takes an item and presents it in a way that helps us decide its value. Marketing assigns value to peoples' physical appearance, objects, events, beliefs, thoughts, organizations, etc. The list is larger but these few will suffice. The world of marketing helps companies make fortunes from these created values because people chase after everything that marketing presents to them. More important than that, what does it tell us about humanity and our worldly values? With all that we can get in this world, we are still not happy. We still battle the voice of the demonic in our minds in our quest to be complete and to fill our wants. The result is a message about this human value system. The system is broken.

The Bible is a big book. It contains a lot of useful data. Jesus' Sermon on the Mount[77] is considered one of the greatest teachings in history. There are nine "make happy" statements. That is literally what beatitude means in Latin. These statements also contain nine rewards or results from these actions or concepts. Jesus

---

[77] Matthew Chapter 5-7

was offering us a look at God's value system. Most people feel that this sermon has some practical advice. The reason is this value system was hardwired into us. Like the receptors that trigger allergies, these values trigger our conscience. We experience sympathy and empathy because of these truths. This is where the Holy Spirit becomes a force of assistance to us. This is where we form the link to the unseen, much like crossing a bridge. These values are not religious values, they are relational values triggering awareness of this guidance from the Holy Spirit and beckoning our freewill to choose compassion, mercy, and forgiveness. But the freewill of broken human's compromises conscience and Holy Spirit guidance. Religion takes advice such as, "there is good for the merciful for they shall receive mercy" and amends it to mean "mercy in certain circumstances". For example, religion has taken topics such as abortion and being gay and turned them into political fights. These are very complex issues because they involve broken human beings, such as those who lie. Yet, all are God's creation. What needs to occur is a conversation between the individual and the Holy Spirit, but religion replaces that meeting. It gives the impression that God is against these people because they are outside God's Will. God knows we are broken. The Father sent Jesus to deliver us from the penalty of the acts we commit while broken. Religion simply has us focused on others' brokenness, not our own. Jesus sent the Holy Spirit to communicate forgiveness and request that we embrace the same attitude[78].

God purposefully meant brokenness to happen[79]. There goes that sovereignty again! The Sermon on the Mount is a teaching that touches those receptors that can help us learn God's ways. Our conscience was not given to us to determine right from wrong. If so, we would really be computers. It was given to us to develop the proper values, the proper attitude. The knowledge of good and evil is not the goal, values are! This is where the demonic deceived Eve and can still deceive us. We cannot escape brokenness in this life but, we can minimize its effect through values and attitude.

---

[78] And so, as those who have been chosen of God, holy and beloved, put on a heart of compassion, kindness, humility, gentleness and patience; [13] bearing with one another, and forgiving each other, whoever has a complaint against anyone; just as the Lord forgave you, (Col 3:12-13 NAS)

[79] For the creation was subjected to futility, not of its own will, but because of Him who subjected it, (Rom 8:20 NAS

Conscience was given to us to determine value[80]. Without a value system, the creation cannot stand[81], neither in this realm or the next. It appears everything about this life ends with death but since there is another realm, the realm of reality[82], value stretches beyond the border of temporal existence and crosses with us. Learning value is paramount because it teaches humility, compassion, and forgiveness. The voice of the Holy Spirit teaches us value if we will listen. These values are not determined by God, they are determined "in" God, since God fills everything. What is valuable exists for all eternity because God exists. Eternal security encompasses these values, and it encompasses all those within the value system. Developing and following these values is hard, yet it is imperative because we must bring these values with us to the next realm. This is where religion fails[83] because

---

[80] "But lay up for yourselves treasures in heaven, where neither moth nor rust destroys, and where thieves do not break in or steal [21] for where your treasure is, there will your heart be also. (Mat 6:20-21 NAS)

[81] "And everyone who hears these words of Mine, and does not act upon them, will be like a foolish man, who built his house upon the sand. [27] "And the rain descended, and the floods came, and the winds blew, and burst against that house; and it fell, and great was its fall." (Mat 7:26-27 NAS)

[82] By faith we understand that the worlds were prepared by the word of God, so that what is seen was not made out of things which are visible. (Heb 11:3 NAS)

[83] "Many will say to Me on that day, 'Lord, Lord, did we not prophesy in Your name, and in Your name cast out demons, and in Your name perform many miracles?' [23] "And then I will

it replaces God's values for human doctrine. Creation cannot exist without the "make happy" statements because creation cannot exist without God. These words I am writing will not speak to your mind, they will speak to your being, your inner spirit person. You will not recognize them by right and wrong, good, and evil. You will recognize them by value, inner fulfilling value, eternal value because they teach what and who to value, even when it appears some others have no value because they disagree with us. This value system is more than words, it is experience, it is relationship, and it is the filling of the void of human aloneness[84] and slowly repairing the state of human brokenness project by project that will culminate with our completeness when The King rewards us. Read the Sermon on the Mount[85] and make your link to the Holy Spirit and the next realm. He is your eternal security and the more you know Him the more you will be secure.

---

declare to them, 'I never knew you; depart from Me, you who practice lawlessness.' (Mat 7:22-23 NAS)

[84] Blessed are the pure in heart, for they will see God. (Mat 5:8)

[85] Sermon on the Mount Matthew Chapter 5 through 7

Takers and Givers

Not everyone may be cognizant of our longing for eternal security as an ongoing thought process but, almost everything we do oozes its juice. The most obvious sign is our passion for life and the lives of those we love. We have discovered many chemicals and practices that will lengthen life, and humanity is living longer. But a long life without employing God's values is a wasted life. There are people who cannot accept the idea of the forgiveness Jesus provided on the cross because it might apply to humans who have committed evil acts. Especially when those acts were experienced personally. The serial killer Ted Bundy, prior to his execution, was ridiculed by some along with his interviewer Dr. James Dobson for attaching something holy, human deliverance, to something evil. Most people wonder how God could forgive the evil committed by such individuals. Evil steals, kills and destroys[86], it takes! Without value, broken humans are takers. What is taken often detracts from the real human problem, the act of taking. This problem is centered on attitude and values. The Sermon on the Mount is for

---

[86] "The thief comes only to steal, and kill, and destroy; I came that they might have life, and might have *it* abundantly (Joh 10:10 NAS)

givers, and for forgivers. Value yields givers and givers yield value. My concern in this life is to learn how to value all that with which I come in contact. This cannot be accomplished unless I see human brokenness. We cannot see this brokenness unless we see it through the eyes of the Holy Spirit. Vengeance is for God, and it will occur[87]. If a human chooses vengeance, they fail at value and possibly at eternal security. Eternal security exists because the words of The King exist, and they exist inside people as companionship with the Holy Spirit. Eternal security is the experience of givers, not takers. Giving oneself is not a place, it is a relationship, a state of being. The words of the Holy Spirit are alive and active[88] every day for those individuals, and their security is linked to them. They recognize value because it exists in God and is spoken to them daily by the Holy Spirit. Religion simply cannot accomplish this task because it gives credit for loving those who love us[89]! Don't be a taker.

---

[87] Never take your own revenge, beloved, but leave room for the wrath *of God*, for it is written, "Vengeance is Mine, I will repay," says the Lord. (Rom 12:19 NAS)

[88] For the word of God is living and active and sharper than any two-edged sword, and piercing as far as the division of soul and spirit, of both joints and marrow, and able to judge the thoughts and intentions of the heart. (Heb 4:12 NAS)

[89] But I tell you, love your enemies and pray for those who persecute you, [45] that you may be children of your Father in heaven. He causes his sun to rise on the evil and the good, and sends rain on the righteous and the unrighteous. [46] If you love those who love you, what reward will you get? Are not even the tax collectors doing that?

Jesus and Paul's Warnings

I understand that people may disagree with my position on organizations but, there are three substantial biblical warnings from the Apostle Paul concerning the effect of organizations. There are also instances in the Tanakh where the people rejected God for organization. Lastly, Jesus himself made a profound statement about his disciples' attachment to religion. Let us consider these examples and the warning attached to them.

1. The earliest was when it was time for Moses to die. The Israelites were about to enter the Promised Land. Moses warned them that they would reject God's relationship and follow other religious organizations and other gods[90].

2. In the book of Samuel, God offers His personal leadership. The people rejected this relationship for an earthly organization and an earthly king[91]. They wanted to be like the other nations. They

---

[90] For I know how rebellious and stiff-necked you are. If you have been rebellious against the LORD while I am still alive and with you, how much more will you rebel after I die! (Deu 31:27 NIV)

[91] And the LORD said to Samuel, "Listen to the voice of the people in regard to all that they say to you, for they have not rejected you, but they have rejected Me from being king over them. (1Sa 8:7 NAS)

chose Saul as their King because he looked the part.

3. Paul speaks at length to the Ephesian group concerning the damage organizational leaders will do in the future[92]. This has been repeated within Christianity for millennia.

4. The next instance occurs when Paul rebukes the Corinthian gathering for following the principles of demonic influence which was breaking them apart. They were assigning honor to men and dividing the people. This organizational influence had the people choosing earthly leaders over Jesus[93] and over the voice of the Holy Spirit.

5. Lastly, and most unsettling, was to the Corinthians. Paul said that even Satan himself[94] masquerades as an angel of light. The demonic realm can masquerade as a good and godly religion.

---

[92] "I know that after my departure savage wolves will come in among you, not sparing the flock; [30] and from among your own selves men will arise, speaking perverse things, to draw away the disciples after them. (Act 20:29-30 NAS)

[93] Now I mean this, that each one of you is saying, "I am of Paul," and "I of Apollos," and "I of Cephas," and "I of Christ." (1Co 1:12)

[94] But what I am doing, I will continue to do, that I may cut off opportunity from those who desire an opportunity to be regarded just as we are in the matter about which they are boasting. [13] For such men are false apostles, deceitful workers, disguising themselves as apostles of Christ. [14] And no wonder, for even Satan disguises himself as an angel of light. (2Co 11:12-14 NAS)

Then there was a warning from Jesus himself when his disciples drew his attention to the magnificence of the Jewish Temple[95]. But Jesus told them it would be dismantled piece by piece. Jesus knows humanity is enamored by religion because of what it represents. We must keep our focus as the Holy Spirit leads us.

I understand that my position may be troubling, but religion silences the voice of the Holy Spirit. Religion itself should be troubling. God is always validating His desire for one-on-one relationship through the voice of the Holy Spirit. Consider the following chapter.

---

[95] And as He was going out of the temple, one of His disciples said to Him, "Teacher, behold what wonderful stones and what wonderful buildings!" [2] And Jesus said to him, "Do you see these great buildings? Not one stone shall be left upon another which will not be torn down." (Mar 13:1-2 NAS)

For The Record

I met a young man recently. He had found Jesus, the right Jesus. Let me share his journey, and why I say the right Jesus. He was brought up in a mainline Christian denomination. His religious exposure was nominal. Yet, he felt he wanted to get closer to God. His father bought him a bible. As he began to read the bible, at the same time he began to search the internet for more answers. There was no pastor, leader, youth group, friend, relative or any other person prompting him. It was the Holy Spirit beckoning him. He found God with the help of God. So did his parents. God wants direct contact and as promised, He does guide people.

When I was a younger man, I would have thought God sent this young man to me to divert him from the dangers of religion and organizations. This is not so anymore. This young man is in God's hands. So, let me continue the story. This young man is now attending a church. As I was speaking to him, he said, "everyone should be in a fellowship". So, I asked him, "does fellowship necessarily mean organization?" He responded, "not necessarily". I then explained to him that he should stay exactly where he was, but he should remember that God's personal contact came before joining the organization. He should not exchange the relationship that guided him to Jesus for membership in some organization. He nodded in agreement.

This young man's experience is an example of all I have written and a validation of the voice of the Holy Spirit in life. If you don't think you have the kind of relationship this young man experienced, then I suggest you pursue one with the Holy Spirit. The internet is a dark place for humanity, yet God used it for good in this young man's life and unlike Pharoah, he responded to the light presented to him. God became his navigator. Don't ever exchange relationship with the Holy Spirit for membership in an organization or the Sunday morning mob.

The Axe and the Root

There was a Jewish man named Yohanan. He was a prophet, a great prophet and no one born was greater than him[96] but he was the humblest, the least of mankind in attitude. He pointed people to change direction and walk away from worldly values because the Messiah was coming. His recognition came from Jesus. This man was his cousin, known to us as John the Baptist. John faced off with the leaders of the organization[97]. He did not start a rebellion against Rome but against human brokenness. This would not free the Jews from Roman oppression, but it would free them from the oppression of the hopelessness of being broken

---

[96] Truly I tell you, among those born of women there has not risen anyone greater than John the Baptist; yet whoever is least in the kingdom of heaven is greater than he. (Mat 11:11 NIV)

[97] But when he saw many of the Pharisees and Sadducees coming to where he was baptizing, he said to them: "You brood of vipers! Who warned you to flee from the coming wrath? 8 Produce fruit in keeping with repentance.

9 And do not think you can say to yourselves, 'We have Abraham as our father.' I tell you that out of these stones God can raise up children for Abraham. 10 The ax is already at the root of the trees, and every tree that does not produce good fruit will be cut down and thrown into the fire.

11 "I baptize you with water for repentance. But after me comes one who is more powerful than I, whose sandals I am not worthy to carry. He will baptize you with the Holy Spirit and fire. 12 His winnowing fork is in his hand, and he will clear his threshing floor, gathering his wheat into the barn and burning up the chaff with unquenchable fire."
(Mat 3:7-12 NIV)

and separate from God. He was sent by the Holy Spirit[98] to prepare the way, the hearts of the people, for the Messiah. He taught and preached about repentance, literally a change of mind, a change of values. He told the people to turn away from human brokenness and walk according to the ways of God. Those ways were found in the Holy Scriptures of Israel, the Bible, and he pointed them toward wholeness by rebuking humanities rebellion against God. Yes, humanity rebels against God every day. But God has a path for us, a path that John pointed toward. The path is Jesus the Messiah, and he came to deliver humanity from their rebellion and bring peace with The Father[99]. God the Father offered an olive branch in His Son Jesus. Jesus became the instrument of our peace by his death and the deliverer of the Fire of the Holy Spirit[100]. The fire that leads to personal conviction and personal change.

---

[98] Finally they said, "Who are you? Give us an answer to take back to those who sent us. What do you say about yourself?" 23 John replied in the words of Isaiah the prophet, "I am the voice of one calling in the wilderness, 'Make straight the way for the Lord.' (Joh 1:22-23 NIV).

[99] "Glory to God in the highest heaven, and on earth peace to those on whom his favor rests." (Luk 2:14 NIV)

[100] "I baptize you with water for repentance. But after me comes one who is more powerful than I, whose sandals I am not worthy to carry. He will baptize you with the Holy Spirit and fire. (Mat 3:11 NIV)

John says the axe lies at the root of each tree[101]. We are the trees, individuals that the Holy Spirit will love individually. We have been given the ability to bear fruit as human beings. That fruit is up to you.

---

[101] "10 "Even now the axe lies at the root of the trees. So that every tree that does not bring forth good fruit is cut down and cast into the fire. (Mat3:10)

Answers to Your Questions

Jesus answered all the questions put to him. They are recorded in the Messianic Writings (New Testament). He has answers for your questions, and they will come through the Holy Spirit[102]. The responses of the Holy Spirit are not like those of religion. They are not universal; they are personal and individual. You do not need an interpreter because the Holy Spirit speaks your language. People have told me the bible is hard to understand. That is because religion has taught you to believe this lie by its dogma and doctrines. Then there are those who would void the bible entirely. That is because they fear the relationship aspect of God's offering. Deitrich Bonhoeffer said it best, The Bible is not a book you read, it is a book of which you make inquires[103]. The answers are provided by the Holy Spirit.

---

[102] "But when He, the Spirit of truth, comes, He will guide you into all the truth; for He will not speak on His own initiative, but whatever He hears, He will speak; and He will disclose to you what is to come. (Joh 16:13 NAS)

[103] "You don't just read the Bible, you must inquire of it.
Metaxas, Eric. Bonhoeffer: Pastor, Martyr, Prophet, Spy. Nashville: Thomas Nelson Publishing, 2010

Go ahead, ask a genuine question, and then wait for the answer[104][105].

Yeshua said to him, you have said it. Yet I tell you that after this you shall see the Son of Adam sitting at the right hand of the Power [PS110:1] and coming on the clouds of the heavens" [Dan. 7:13]

Mat 26:64[106]

---

[104] "Ask, and it shall be given to you; seek, and you shall find; knock, and it shall be opened to you. (Mat 7:7 NAS)

[105] "But seek first His kingdom and His righteousness; and all these things shall be added to you. (Mat 6:33 NAS)

[106] Gruber, Daniel. *The Separation of Church and Faith.* Hanover: Elijah Publishing, 2005.pp63

More Info: www.thehouseofbread.com
John's Books

He Will Guide You
Truth, Experience the Holy Spirit

Know My Voice I
The Mystery of the Thread of Israel

Know My Voice II
God Has a Kingdom and it is not Organized Religion

Know My Voice III
The Insanity of Humanity

Know My Voice IV
Marriage, Commitment, Responsibility, Relationship, Intimacy, Choice

Know My Voice V
The Jesus You Never Met

Know My Voice VI
Life, Death, Hope
The Journey to the Next Realm

Know My Voice VII
The King, The Kingdom, The Citizens
Recognizing and Entering The Kingdom

Know My Voice VIII
Christianity, Religion, Deception
The Process of Recognizing, Choosing and Obeying

www.ingramcontent.com/pod-product-compliance
Lightning Source LLC
Chambersburg PA
CBHW050008040726
47599CB00014B/1269